POEMS, RHYMES

REAL FOUL MOUTHED SHIT!

GEORGE

authorHOUSE

AuthorHouse™
1663 Liberty Drive
Bloomington, IN 47403
www.authorhouse.com
Phone: 1 (800) 839-8640

Published by AuthorHouse 03/03/2020

ISBN: 978-1-7283-4961-9 (sc)
ISBN: 978-1-7283-4960-2 (e)

Print information available on the last page.

Contents

Introduction

This magnificent book is a catastrophe of words spun
together to make you laugh and cry til you shit yourself
blind, but sadly, there's a more pressing issue at hand
then your need for plenty of toilet paper and fresh jeans-
we need to address the elephant in the room and I'm
not talking about your sister, the fat fuck that she is;
This is the third book in the poem series* and if you
haven't already purchased and read the other two... that
makes you a filthy, dirty, selfish, shitwhore who doesn't
care if my children get fed. They're fucking starving, but
just as long as you're entertained, that's all that matters,
right? It's people like you that I wish would shit in a
canoe. That's right, everyone else was afraid to say it, but
I'm going to call it like I see it. Go shit in a canoe, with
no shoes, maybe in flip flops, so when the shit drops, you
slip and fall in it, accidentally kicking it, making you a
canoe shitkicker. And that is just the worst fucking thing
I can imagine. Someone who kicks shit in a canoe?
Oh my god. Just awful.

Hope you enjoy what's been written. It's a good
mix. They're not all jokes about your grandfather's
shriveled cock, but most of the poems are extremely
offensive to the average pussy. You've been warned.

I wanted to share all of the 'Dirtier' poems of the
three book series, in one book. So you'll notice, near
the end, six poems were gathered from the first
and second books and are now also at home in this
collection as well as in their original printing.

*Poems, Rhymes & Real Heartfelt Shit
**Poems, Passages & Real Heartfelt Shit
***Poems, Rhymes & Real Foul Mouthed Shit

Santa's Coming

Go back to sleep little one, It's Christmas Eve and I'm going in deep. Not a creature was stirring except this dick in my jeans. I see your mother sleeping in those lacy red panties, ass up in a dream. I ate the warm cookies, I laid out the scene under the tree, now it's time to eat that ass and fill your mother's pretty bottom with sweet Christmas cream.
Rudolph my red tipped penis, won't
you guide my lay tonight.
So hang those stockings and go back to bed, and let your sisters over 21, know to keep their doors open instead. I'll check my lists, I'll check them twice, but not before I go balls deep in their asses tonight.

Desiree

Oh Desiree, you far-sighted slut. Your eyes are so far apart, it looks like your mother fucked an alien then ran you over with a truck. But here's the amazing part and its not just me, there's a whole town saying,
"If you can just get past the spread on her head, her pussy is as fresh as warm baked summer bread. Shaven and sweet, it's a delight and a treat to cum in that seam. Just don't look up at the freak with the 'E.T.' glance, one look and it'll scare your cock right back into your pants."

Three Goats and a Duck

Three goats fucked a duck. It's just that simple. I
wish it were grander in fashion and tale, but this is
the true story at hand. Allow me to expand. It was
all kinds of fucked up, not a female in the bunch.
The duck flat out agreed to fuck all three goats after
lunch if he lost the bet. "I'm dead set on this bet." the
goat said, "If my head can fit in this ducks rear end,
then we three shall hump his rump til we're spent.
Fred, the duck, said,
"Be my guest, you'll never get your head up my ass, friend."
So Fred reached for his toes, touched the floor
with his nose and waited for the goat to choke.
Suddenly the duck felt hands on his hips and
a hairy dick fit into his feathery rump.
"Hey that's not your head, chump."
The goat replied with a pump, "The hell it's not, I never
said which head, now take a deep breath and keep
your cheeks tight, it's gonna be a long fuckin' night."

Pepper the Cock

This is not a recipe to make dick taste better or season a man's member. And it's certainly not a way to spice up that boring shit you call a love life. No, this is about a rooster named Pepper. Pepper was hard headed, some say he was a thick cock. He'd walk around like he owned the place, like a big shot. Head held high, a real cock of the walk. Until one day a chicken moved in, her name was Tittania. "Hello boy." she said, "Names Tittania. But you can call me Titts for short. I'll have you know I'm the boss around here so they call me Big Titts."
Well, Pepper was not happy, in fact you could say he was an angry cock, who wanted to choke that chicken til she dropped.
The next day he saw Big Titts trying to fit into a shirt after she put on a skirt.
"Well who does she think she is?" Pepper said, "Big Titts in a skirt? That's preposterous, so he went up and poked her and told her, "I'm the Big boss, I'm the Big cock and I call the shots. I don't like you wearing a dress!" Big Titts got right in his face. And that's when he saw her pretty eyes and realized he loved Big Titts. In fact he loved Big Titts in a shirt, he loved Big Titts in a skirt.

"Listen Big cock," she said. "I own you. I tell you what to do, and for the rest of your life you'll make me happy or I'll beat you until you cry all over your crusty socks. Pepper the cock submitted and rested his head on her breasts. And that's the day Pepper the cock learned, he loved Big Titts in a dress.

Bubble Boy

The boy in the bubble got into so much trouble for
eating his food so fast. In a way, it gave him such
obnoxious gas, it drove his mother insane.
"It's the sound that bothers me most."
she said as she ate her toast.
"It's the thought of butt cheeks slapping like Canadian
geese clapping on a busy broken highway."

"Look, I fart everyday, I've farted 4 million times in my
lifetime and I'll keep eating this way. I can't stop the gas
that passes through my ass or I'll be in a lot of pain.
If you don't like my farts, just go away.
Be grateful they're just air that don't leave stains or
you'd be cleaning up a couch full of shit where I ate."

Coming to the Big Screen

Downward I count and onward I travel through world's
that unravel their mystery and story. A fun meal to go,
some cushions to soften the blow and my ass is planted
firmly. The music blares, the giant screen glares and I'm
whisked into the saga I can't wait to know. Home alone, I
dim the lights, feeling excited and chipper. I lean back to
kick off my boots and undo my pants zipper, but it seems
to be stuck, and now with every buck, it's not coming
undone, only frayed and torn and pissing me off even
more, because today was my only day to jack off to porn.

<u>Junkie</u>

It's the fiend that does you in, that crawls into your
skin, like demons choking you from within.
You let the poison in, craving the chemicals that
change you. Slowly starving the miracle that is you.
It's the evil in the drug that defines you, making you
do things you'd never thought you'd ever fucking do.
You'll steal from your own father, offer it to your
own brother, curse out your sisters and mother and
shut out the world around you. You poison your
body and sell your soul just to get high one more
time which you swear in your mind is the real last
time and this time you mean it, even though
you know you can't beat it alone.
You've sold off everything you owned, betrayed
everyone you know, including yourself. You've
lost every friend, at wit's end, buried your
brother, but when and where does it end?
You hangout with the worst kind of people, in filthy
dirty in places, on dark streets staring at diseased
faces, broke and alone, broken to the bone. Windows
of opportunity knock on your door that you continue
to ignore, lying to yourself, saying they'll be more.
lying on the floor, you can't take anymore.

And then you breakdown crying,
in lying, dirty hands stained with all your broken plans.
You know deep down in your heart you threw away a
great life possibly with a great wife and kids and now
God's pissed and crying at the same time, watching
you slowly die with your own soul torn apart.

You beg for forgiveness with all you got
and hope for one last fresh start.

5

My Friend Wang

My friend Wang is of Chinese descent. You pricks
thought this was a poem about my dick, but it isn't.
It's people like you you who sit around with their
mind in the gutter, thinkin about who's fuckin who's
mother. It's pure, filthy, perverted scumbaggery.
Is this what you think of me?
Like oh that's so funny, some fuckin Chinese
guy with a tiny dick, sittin in a tree, yelling,
"Me so horny".
Well my friends, I'm sorry but Wang is my buddy
and there's nothing to tell. We don't sit around
suckin' each others dicks for the hell of it.
We're grown men with bills to pay.
We do it for money-
Fie dolla, sucky sucky.

Bum Rush

It's a particular love to pump the glove that
bares the look of a birthday-balloon's knot.
It's said, once you pack that ass, there's no
turning back cuz nothing else feels as hot.
If you ask, then I must attest to the best
finish I ever had. What can I say?
She loved the attention I gave her bottom
and it kinda made her blush.
When I finally came in her bum
it was glorious fun that made both
my arms and legs go numb.
And that is why,
I always try to find a girl who isn't shy
about taking it in the butt.

Tight AF

Look, every guy cries how he wants a tight twat- like it's
the greatest thing in the world's pussybook. Now don't
misunderstand, a tight vag is grand, and the book was
written by hand, way back when cock was in demand,
but if a pussy's too tight, it's like a squeegee to the shaft
on the way out making it dry and harder to slide back
in. Unless your dick is really thin and your name is
clit-prick or 'needle-dick the bug fucker'
and you can hug fuck a tin cup on a bug's butt in Lubbock
with a crew cut and a sac o' nuts, then stack your nuts, like
jenga blocks, like astronauts with a bag of dicks, floating
around the dock, a fuckin laughing stock with a tiny cock;
Then you too, will find it hard to bang the lips betwixt
her hips if the opening is too thin.
Personally, Id rather ride her chin and
rest my balls on her grin.
Then there's no fight to get in.

Deep Poetry, Deep in your Mama's Ass

I want you to know while you're in school coloring
rainbows and picking your nose I go deep in your mama's
ass, curling her fuckin' toes. Oh I know you play this
game at five years old where she's always gotta be up your
ass, or you'll throw a fit, but look here ya little shit, since
you're daddy left, your mama's been needin' that dick, so
go take a bath, go to your little fuckin' karate class, cuz
when your not here or asleep dreamin' of jellybeans and
he-man dolls, I'm pumpin' the fuck out of your mother's
sweet ass while she's on all fours, making her scream
my name til she forgets yours. Now go play in traffic.

Simple Simon

Simple Simon knew of the hymen, he just didn't know
how to please it. He left a note, begging his friends to
help him locate and tease it. Finally, he had no choice
but to practice alone on his teddybear that sat on the
end of his bed. He practiced for hours a day, battling
the fur, giving the stuffed animal fantastic head.
Then Betty, the girl he wanted to please,
came over his house later that week.
He told her to get undressed and wait in his
bed for the best thing she'd ever get.
Simon showed up with a glove and a bucket
prompting Betty to ask why, leaving Simon to reply;
I'm going to give you the best lickin you ever had.
To which they'll be no stoppin'
I just have to get down between your legs
and get rid of all that fuckin cotton.

Happy Feet

Diana wasn't all that pretty, but she wasn't all the bad
either. Still, the boys wouldn't chase her or ask to date
her, instead they would all just fucking tease her.
While Diana grew up hot as fuck and became a woman
blessed with luck, the clueless boys grew tall with
balls and became a bunch of degenerate fucks.

Diana had a great look with a fine body, but the men
were entranced over something else it would seem. She
followed their stare and caught them taking a liking to
the oddest of all, her feet. Curious and inquisitive in
nature she asked a gentleman what was the big deal.

"Madame," he exclaimed. "they are perfect in size,
in the sexiest of high heels that compliment your
magnificent thighs. Also with an ankle choker in design
and a naked instep, they display the perfect curves of
your foot and high arches. And your toes are equally
the show, like beautiful Christmas snow, painted and
trimmed wonderfully in lilac purple and gold."

"Um, ok, but what does that mean to me, you
weird, sick fuck?"
Without hesitation, the man replied,
"About five hundred and fifty bucks."
And from that day on, everyone knows, Diana made
bank off the sick pricks that loved to fuck her toes.

Dear Fuckhole Shitwhore

Dear Fuckhole Shitwhore, and I mean
this in the nicest possible way.
Why the fuck do you want me to bash
your teeth in with a crowbar?
Why are you begging me to get out of my car,
thus far, and beat you so fucking hard you'd have
to change your medical card to retard...
I don't understand your logic, you rather get punched
in the dick than to use that little lever that makes a
click on the side of your steering wheel's stick?
Well here's a neat trick.
The next motherfucker that doesn't let me know
he's making a left by using his turn signal,
I'm going to shove my foot so far up his ass,
he'll taste leather in the back of his throat and
cough up shoe laces til he chokes, while my foot
becomes a permanent part of his stinker.
Now go fuck yourself and use your god dam blinker!

Bathroom Epiphany

I came up with an idea.
It's seems to be unavoidable.
The idea came to me,
as I was sitting on the toilet bowl.
My balls hanging low;
shit was flowing like a river from my soul, or maybe it was
the Tabasco, I suppose we'll never truly know, but
I must say, my asshole never fails to deliver.
Anyway, the idea was so bright
and had so much fucking flavor
I decided to write it down on the last bit of toilet paper.
After I was done,
I was a little in shock.
Should I use my idea
or use my sock?
Since the explosion was so severe it became quite clear,
use the paper to wipe the remnants from my rear.

Now, if I could only remember what the fuck was my idea.

Junkie II

A few things are clear.
Some clearer than others. Some become
clear as the days become drawn.
Girls give no love, it's something only a
woman can. Regardless, I've moved on.
No one cares about an old-school junkie. Not even
sure what that means, I've labeled myself like I'm
diseased. Maybe I am. I'm definitely infected and
the pill bottle designed to protect me and resurrect me
is fucking killing me. But what isn't. Nights kill me. Days
kill me. Memories haunt me, hurt me, remind me.
Time taunts me.
And 'purity is clarity' they say. Even that remains
questionable. Seeing things more clearly can be a
prison, trapped alone with the decisions and truths
that I have done to myself and others- have created
the isolation in which I now suffer in sobriety.
Withdrawals are the warden.
And my dick... The last insignificant joke that
constantly reminds my heart of what I miss most;
her close,
my name synonymous with trust.
I single-handedly fucked that up.
In vision I see the love I'll never see again.
Alone I sit. Waiting for energy to decide on
whether or not my life's worth fighting for.
I've entertained a demon for too long... but how do I go
on after all that I've done. Oh god what have I done.
Am I done?
This collision with conscience
This revision
An executive decision.
Hmm.
Do I even give a fuck to keep on livin'.

Wise Man Said

Obsession always ends in a lesson of pain.
obsessed with war, with love, with financial gain,
at the end of the day, they all end the same.
heartbroken, torn and frayed. Be wary of your
obsession, its a time bomb ticking away.

Wealth is never your friend. wealth is not
about money kept or spent, it's about the depth
of your investment, will it last til the end.

Sacrifice must be made, it's literally the name of
the game and the key to success. Sacrifice is how
you make room for a better way. Something's gotta
give and it's usually the highest on the list and tied
with the best choice of what not to let go of.

Love is amazing in all its glory, but it's better kept on
the lower tiers such as adoration and respect. Once you
label it love, you can't take it back. Enjoy it while you
can, and don't put all your eggs in this one basket.
It won't last and always comes to an end.

A wealthy man could be a poor man rich in
love. But love won't last forever. Now, his
obsession got the best of him and the sacrifices
he made took away any alternate life he could've
had with the things he pushed away.

Steel and Stone

One day it'll say on my cold lifeless grave;
"Here lies a man that never gave up."

Courageous and brave or a fools plight.
When is it ok to give up the good fight.
But if it's nothing but fights and there's nothing
left to save, then why stick it out?
You can keep trying, but eventually
you have to ask yourself;
How many times have we tried, cried and nearly died.
And, if the house won't stand then burn it down.
After we're free and we walk, are we though?
And at what cost?
We're not the only ones who've lost.
Do we just go on, carrying on, leaving the fires
burning behind us? like nothing happened?
I think the answer is yes and simply- move on.
The fires will eventually burn out, and when they're
long gone, I'm going back to rebuild what there was.
The idea was there, the foundation just needs to be
built with more care. In fact, it'll be better than before,
sturdier than earth and bone, and stronger than
Steel and Stone.
I'll never give up on my heart's home.

Reflection

Everyone has been a victim, so let's not carry on
like a whiny cunt and fuck up our day. Been there,
done that, We've all felt the fucking pain.
To the master, one way or another, we become it's slave.
Personally, I'm tired of working at it, looking for it. Tired
of waking up distracted, retracted, over critical, miserable,
self-dissected, over obsessive, and aggressively looking
over my shoulder in fear of missing out on the entrance to
my salvation, yet again. How many chances can one get.
I know it's a long shot but it's a bet I believe in and yes,
I hope that it's not such a beat down this time around.
It comes but it doesn't stay, it never does, so is it worth
the frayed sanity, loss of dignity, the kiss of death
straight through the heart of me? How we forget
so easily. I'm literally shaking my head, *at* me.
Still, I pray that it may be right around the corner. A
fresh start. That, I hold close to my heart. It seems
to get me through the dark cursed days. But I'm still
afraid of the way I acted and the way I became. I'm
afraid of the cliche pain and the fucking weakening
drain it's tailwinds of misery claim in it's wake.
So, I'll refrain. Are you truly ready
to tangle with love again?

6 Dicks for Jimmy

Jimmy was a peculiar child and not like the rest,
making it hard for the wish foundation and really
putting them to test. Although he was sick, Jimmy
had just one wish; to meet 6 Dicks before his time
was dead. "Jimmy your request is rather unorthodox",
they said. "and I'm not sure we can meet it."
Jimmy insisted on 6 dicks. Not 5, not 4, he
wanted all 6 Dicks and nothing more.
He loved the dicks so much he'd often pretend he was a
Dick going to work. "Can you see me mother? I'm a Dick.
A glorious famous handsome Dick. I wanna make movies
like the ones all those Dicks are in. I wanna be a household
name and hear Dick coming out of everyone's mouth.
"Jimmy what is your infatuation with all these dicks?"
"Mother, they're splendid, they're terrific,
I've always started my day with a Dick! I
think my favorite is the black dick!"
Jimmy's mother sat on the bed curious
about the dicks in Jimmy's head.
"Have you seen these dicks?" She said.
Oh everyday. I pretend I'm a dick even when I play.
"Jimmy I don't know what to say," she said to her
dismay. Then Jimmy gave his mother a list,
"It's a dick checklist."
1. Dick Van Dyke 4. Dick York
2. Dick Van Patton 5. Dick Clark
3. Dick Van Horn 6. Richard Roundtree

although he goes by Richard he's still a dick to
me and the only black dick in the bunch.

Elated, Jimmy's mother let out her breath.
"That black Dick *was* the best Jimmy,
but I think these Dicks are dead."
"Just give them Viagra mommy, that's what
Daddy said last night in your bed."
"This pill will wake up any dick, even one that's dead".

Your Mother has a Horse Cock

"... Hello? Yeah it's me.
Whats up? Ok, I'll tell you. Bottom line, I caught her
in the act. I saw some shit I wish I could give back.
What do you mean '*who*'?
You're fucking mom, THAT'S fucking who.
Anyway, YOU'RE fucking mom told me to meet her,
so I did. How I found her is not what I expected.
On all fours owning a horse cock like it was
hers. What was she doing? All the shit she
shouldn't be doing to a horse's cock, bro!
I had no idea she was that flexible. Don't get me wrong,
it's downright respectable, but she did things I didn't
know you could do to a regular cock, forget about one
of that magnitude. It was a fucking horse, dude.
Of course it was a horse, where else you gonna find
a cock that size, that dark, that big, that fat...

What do you mean your step dad's black?

Mighty Dreamers

Beneath mighty dreams lie young souls with
excited minds, unbeknownst to the whole
shit show- we call life.
They run wild with energy, using each other's synergy to
chase those vivid scenes of riches and happiness they've
imagined in extravagant detail, thinking we failed and how
they can see things more clearly and know better than we.
These little shits think how we derailed and lost our way.
How we ruined our lives and theirs when we woke up
and just decided, we'd rather work every fucking day.

Let me tell you something little dreamer, I'm happy you
still have that gleam in your eye. Don't lose it, keep it
for awhile. In fact, keep it for as long as you can because
one day you're gonna fuck up and want too much, such
as a place to live, and food in the fridge. You'll want heat
for your kids when its cold and a roof over their heads
when it snows. You're gonna get greedy and give to the
needy. You're gonna get crazy and want a baby, then go
nuts and give everything to that baby you possibly can
to make it happy. But your bills will enslave you and
own you, decades later, you'll be broke and lonely. Then
your kid will spit on you and tell you, you're a fucking
piece of shit that did nothing right in life, if only...

Don't worry, I wont hold it against you.
One day you'll understand
And you can always come to me for advice.
I'm your Dad for life.

Everything's a God dam hassle

I rather fist fuck my own mouth than deal with some of
the unnecessary hassles of the day. Especially if they're
motherfucking outdated and antiquated in any way.
Why the fuck am I still dealing with this shit in
2020, fuck all you all you pieces of shit in charge of
making things faster and better, obviously you've
left out a few things like shoe fucking strings.
I mean, really motherfucker?
You can't permanently get rid of the fucking shoe lace?
We can rocket around the sun and fly planes to fancy
places, but grab a pair of shoes and it's stop what
you're doing to put on these archaic devices.
It's a major fucking hassle, not to mention
uncomfortable. I rather get fucked 9 separate times
by a mountain goat with dick warts that spread,
than deal with lacing shit up with thread.
Because it doesn't stop there. You hurt your finger trying
to get the shoe on, then you're thrown off balance and
knock shit over, you woke up the baby, pulled a muscle
in your back, ripped the lace, hurt your ankle, then
hit your head on the table all while bending down...
It's unfuckingbelievable how much it's a hassle.
Fuck shoes, fuck laces,
don't even get me started on wiping
our asses with balls of paper.

Pussy Farts of the Heart

Ya meant well, so I adore your intention, however
I can't ignore or just forget what ya said,
it's still a fizzling fart that rings out in my head.
Your affection is beautiful in design,
coming from a beautiful mind, with a passion that's
heartfelt and one of a kind and definitely recognized,
but it still slipped out and the words played out a
scene that made me cringe and hold my mouth.
I know you love me, I truly get it,
but please,
let go of the things that can make us uncomfortable
in the things you say. Neither one of us is capable of
time travel or able to fix the mistakes of yesterday.

<u>Your Sister's Fucking Hot</u>

Sorry dude, but your sister's fuckin' hot.
and I'm tellin you now,
I'm gonna bang her whether you like it or not.
Let me explain before you get all worked up.
It was love at first sight when I saw your sister's tits.
I feel like I was struck by cupids arrow...
straight in the dick.
she gives me brick dick whenever I think about her
taking a shit. And if she says hello? forget about it.
When I look at her, things I've never thought of
doing to anyone- just appear in my head.
Scenes of me stuffing her six ways til Sunday play
out like a concerto of pornographic bends.
Honestly? I hope she gives head. Maybe it runs
in the family. I know your mom did way back
when, at least that's what your dad said.
I'll slow gag her, raw dog her,
and show her fifty shades of my taint.
I will make that pussy rain, bro.
That ass is insane though.
And just like the rest of her,
I'm gonna bend her, undress her,
and eat her ass like a pezz dispenser.
I want to lick her like a dog licks asshole in the summer.
Forever.
let's see how it goes... cuz brother,
I'm getting tired of fuckin' your mother.

We still on for dinner?

Fuck the Gutter

You've become a monicker. A beacon to some and for them
you must change the way you're speaking. Adjust your
breathing, don't say anything without fully understanding
you're the reason they're believing. Wipe the slates clean
of hatred no matter how much you're seething. Walk a
mile in anyone else's shoes before you cry the blues and
become yesterday's news. Fuck that and Fuck you! Be the
fucking news. scream and shout. play the entire game
before playing yourself out like a washed up Hollywood
has-been with no modern day clout. Times running out.
How old will you be when you finally figure it all out?
There's a fine line where rhymes rise above words
and become something more that disturb the mind,
dropping anchor in time, penetrating the brain, giving
you strength to fight the rains and downtrodden days.
The clock is ticking, why would you give in? Why
would you wait!? Make your life worth living. Run
til your feet are bleeding, til your fucking shoes are
screaming. Then tell your children that dreaming is
believing in yourself, achieving your goals, and fulfilling
your soul with everything existence has to offer you.
Expect more from you. You can't afford not to.

<u>Pissing in the Wind</u>

It's funny how life works, but it's a fool who thinks it's coincidence. It's the universe working from design specs, carrying out it's plan to dissect, whether we're aware or not, it's in effect. A mere grain of sand in the breadth of time we take our breath. Clueless and selfish, idiotic and restless, inwardly boxed in, fighting for scraps and useless rocks, instead of joining in on exploring the lights that wave us in. We beg the universe to help us in our darkest hour as if we're special and deserve to be saved from the destiny we've created. Then somehow a reprieve comes and for some it's a miracle sent from above and graciously loved, others simply receive and ignore, succumb and take more of the temptations that career our beliefs and spit on the gifts so extraordinarily given and then keep on wishing.

It's a miracle we're still living.

Nothing but Bullshit

It's truly fucking amazing how an Ex can go from
nice and pretty to fuckin bitch and greedy,
wonderful and classy to shithead and nasty,
caring and funny to "Where's my fuckin money".
"I think I love you" to
"How are you this fucking stupid?"

And the feeling is shared by every one who has ever
had an Ex. We all know it and have to deal with it. But
the bewilderment is how it's seen and validated from
either side. It's rare for the one ex to agree they are the
shithead, instead, this is what's said from both sides:

"I don't even know what I ever saw in you. It's been
nothing but bullshit since I left you and unfortunately
I still have to deal with you. You're exhausting,
haunting, climbing into my mind, questioning,
belittling, is it wrong of me wishing you'd die?
I literally can't even tell you how much I
loathe you. How did I ever love you?
You're no longer clever or sweet, not even sure you
ever were to me. You're actually a bad fucking dream,
curdling my stomach and screams. You're a nightmare
on wheels. I shriek and shiver, even puke when you
deliver your newest thoughts and ideas and when you
open your mouth, nothing but the stupidest shit I've
ever heard, pours out. I've had to learn how to ignore
and tune you out, pretend you never existed is really
the name of the game or else the stress of your
existence causes me to go in-fucking-sane."

The 'Ex' . . . Cupid's drunken mistake.

Chinese Peas

This is a not a story about a tiny green vegetable,
regardless of what you think you read in the title, but
rather a pretty Chinese girl who likes to pee on people.

When you think, Chinese, you think of fried rice and
wok greens. You don't think of sweet Asian girls peeing
on peoples feet. Personally, it's not one of my dreams,
I don't sit around fantasizing about girls peeing in
front of me, my feet, the street or on my man meat.
I simply walked in on her accidentally, and
thought she was the cutest thing I'd ever seen.
So to test the waters she stepped inside the
tub and pissed in the shower so I could see
the potent juice pour out of her flower.
But here's where it got weird, as if it weren't quite
the scene already and messed up, yup. If it weren't
for bad luck, I wouldn't have any luck, cuz this is
fucked up; like two girls and one cup chugging butt
muck from a dixie cup. *That* kinda 'fucked up'.

She was a true centerpiece, a sight to see.
She was as beautiful as can be, with tits like
cream and eyes like the sea, but when I say
this, and I mean this respectfully...
She had a keyhole and a key,
a doorknob and a lever, a flower and a bee,
some low hanging fruit from her tree,
a twig and two berries, a snap and two peas,
wood next to her beaver,
both pussy and penis, and I mean this...
even though she was pretty,
her peeing on me, was the least of my fucking worries.

My Sister's a Slut

My sisters a slut, and not cuz she takes it up the butt
or snap chats her fat ass with her ass crack in the tub.
She'll fuck anything that walks, anything that breathes,
she doesn't need a reason, it's always fucking season.
Tom, Dick and Harry, even his dog Larry, and that's
pretty fuckin... weird. I was going to say, weird. You
thought I was going to say *scary*? Well that too.

It's a rarity she'd turn down anyone with a disability,
she's even fucked me, relax, not lately and she's not
blood related, so as I was saying, you could have a
broke leg, snapped back, cracked head, crooked back,
stitched up, bent dick butt chugger, limp dick cock
sucker, blood stained, toe sprain, half a brain, half a
nut, one testicle- up your butt, hit by a Mack truck,
lean lip, broke hip, fat dick, short cock, long dick,
ass wart, foot scratch, crotch rot, dingleberry,
blood clot, loss of family, dual personality,
even if you practice homo-sexuality,
goat fucker, street begger, ass licker, drunken kegger,
drop out, ball-less, spineless, sockless,
cockless, motherless, even that guy from
the movie; Legoles. Hold on I got this.
Big black, short stack, midget dicked, horse-cocked,
jugg fucking, homeless, backstabbing jobless, nose
picker, trash picker, white trash, blacklister. It
doesnt ever stop and it doesn't fuckin matter, she's
even fucked the fire man, on his fuckin ladder.

It's a miracle she don't have any diseases,
praise Jesus.

Space Ace & Monkey II

This is Space Ace. Can anybody hear me? I'm way off
course and clearly, approaching the sun. It's so fucking
hot and i'm so fucking wet, my nuts are deep frying in
ball fucking sweat. My asshole gave out and phoned
the fuck in, I farted so loud I thought I shit twins.
As for monkey, I don't know where he is, but
something smells funky. If he ain't dead in the
back of the ship with clumps of shit floating around
him, then I'm sure he's jacking off, drinking his
piss and humping the steam pipes that hiss.

"Space Ace we hear you, we must tell you, the monkey
can save you. He's been trained to help you fly when
you're lost. The only problem is he can't pshhhh...
his ...pshhhhh... long enough to right your course.
We suggest you help him release... pshhhhh... he...
pshhhhhh... choke ...pshhhh... thing... pshhhh

"You're breaking up mission control, but I'm on a roll.
I did what you said and helped him release. I
played with his thing and choked the monkey
til he came in his seat, but so far he's done
nothing but grin. Seems like I can't win."

"Space Ace are we hearing you correctly? You
jerked off the monkey that's specifically there to
help co-pilot your mission with his training?
I was merely explaining..."

"How he can't let go of his dick?"

"No Space Ace, his seat belt is stuck
and sometimes won't click."

"Oh. Shit."

Shit Luck

I'm telling this story one fucking time, right
now, right here, and the ass fucking that
took place will soon become clear
Is it all luck? I was told it was, and what I did was
to secure a win, with better tactics, so listen closely
you spastic, fat little, video game playing bastards.
I fought a god and here's what happened.
a mighty rumble took place with a man fighting for his life.
What if the storm *does* last all night?
well, it could, so that's why I was ready to prove I
was right. The level of the Devil and his revel were
a forecast of fright. this was going to be one hell of
a motherfuckin fight, but my victory was well in
sight, just as the lyrics of this poem are extremely
tight, or so I think, remember I'm white.
I ran into the storm with a mighty weapon, a bucket
full of clovers, all ready to turn a new leaf over, start
again, cuz this time I had luck on my side. I could
finally hold my head up high. The deal I made with the
Devil was over and he would suck *my* dick this night.

"Fuck you big red!" I would yell.
"I'm coming out like a soldier and I got a new
weapon that'll send you straight to hell!"

The Devil had a look on his face like he knew something
I didn't. I saw it in his eyes as he blazed into mine,
tears began to fall in the heat and crystallize. I begged and
pleaded and suddenly realized who'd be sucking who's dick
tonight. The Devil sneered and said please motherfucker
please, cry me a river then get down on your knees...
That bucket of luck is fucked,
all those clovers have three fuckin leaves."

Award Winning Poem

Into
dark
chasm
thirst
reason
in dry mouth
the
river
doth flow
It twas
my
piss
be it
known.

Grandma's Big Tits

I hate to be that guy. I hate to make a scene or be
obscene, but it seems to me I'm the only one that sees
your grandmother's tits swinging around in the breeze.
Those are some big fuckin titties and no one has said
a word to me, but that's not even what scares me.
I can't seem to look away. I'm both distracted and attracted
to their sway. They're so fucking big and those nipples can
be seen a mile a fucking way, literally anytime of day. Is
it wrong I jerked off thinking about her the other day?
I'm sorry and I know this sounds fucked up, but all I
want is for her to give me a handjob in the bathtub.
Oh don't act like she's a fuckin virgin, she's nurturing,
she's clever, she can even knit me a gay ass sweater.
All I'm sayin is next time we all hang out and
play, just look the other way while I peek through
the keyhole and watch your grandmother bathe
those big ass tits in the middle of the day.

Sally has a bag of Dicks

Some girls like jewelry, some girls crave money,
not sally, she carries a bag of tricks that make her
smile a mile wide wherever she goes, and all who
know her, know she never travels without it.
Happy and horny is one route this could've gone in
the story of sally and her bag of wondrous wrongs,
but tragically, this isn't a happy go lucky skip down the
street, story. No, this has no glory or decency, it's about
a psycho fuck that carries a selection of cutlery and
irrevocably cuts off the dicks of the pricks she humps daily.
"A bag of dicks" isn't a metaphor or a cute bag of rubber
dildos, no, sally is a fuckin lunatic that chops off man
members and stashes them in a bag til she can go
home to make a nicely seasoned soup. So be careful
not to hump the girl with the smiley faced tattoo, or
it could be your dick in her next flavorful stew.

Three Ring Circus

Buckshot Buck

Buckshot Buck McCrit was a retarded little fucking
twit, who got his dick stuck in a duck after he fucked
it in the butt with a grin. His momma came running
outside with her broken toothed smile, and yelled
"Buckshot Buck, you retarded little fuck, what are
you doing with your dick stuck in that duck?"
Buckshot replied with a mighty fucking cluck,
"Just my luck, the duck died. Now I'm dick-stuck in
a dead-duck with a fat-fuck yelling outside, asking
me why my dick's inside this ducks behind. But
since my dick-tip is now a dipstick with a brown
tip saying I'm dick-deep in duck shit, I'm thinking
of changing my name to 'Shitdick McCrit."

Donnie Bo Duck

Donnie Bo was an unlucky little duck who got
fucked in the butt by Buckshot Buck.
"We were stuck in the muck next to his truck
when he snuck his pecker into my butt. So I
yelled, 'Buckshot Buck you redneck schmuck,
get your dick out of my goddam butt!'
That's when his mother, that short fat fuck with her
broken tooth smile who ain't much better than a
convicted pedophile, yelled out some shit while draggin'
her saggin-ass tits across the ground during my
ass-fucking round.
I couldn't really tell what she said, I was too busy
pretending to be dead while Buckshot pumped my butt
full of redneck lead. Well I had always said, they couldn't
be trusted, so I rubbed my ass in poison ivy and mustard
and right now McCrit can scratch his shit covered, itchy-
dick til his prick falls off his skinny ass, redneck hips.

Two-Fingers May McCrit

Names, May McCrit. They call me Two-Fingers
May or Ma, either way, I don't give a shit.
I was just sittin' on the porch mindin' my own business,
drinkin' a shlitz-six when I saw Buckshot treatin'
Donnie Bo like his big sis. I mean what
kind of monkey shit is this!?
So I put down my beer nuts and ran
like diarrhea down a dog's leg.
"Quit fuckin that duck in the rear!" I yelled hard.
"It's flat out queer, ya goddam retard.

The truth is, Buckshot Buck ain't that smart. He got
his name when he got shot in the back-room of a hock-
shop with salt-rock from fucking a dumb-twat without
a cock-sock. The boyfriend, her brother, broke their
lip-lock, put Buck in a headlock and blasted his ass
one-handed. Left ole Buck stranded with salt
rocks in his ham hock, so I went fingers deep to
sweep out the grit stuck in Buck's ass meat.
And even to this day, they still call me
Two-Fingers May.

Not Even 6 Dicks Could Save Jimmy

Lil jimmy the sick boy who loved Dicks,
had an incurable illness.
(Obviously it was incurable or we wouldn't be
talking about his lifeless ass and how he's pushing
up daisies at 12 years of age. just saying.)
Now lil jimmy would want us to rejoice and go on, not
dwell on the fact that he's a stiff, six feet under, who
shamelessly put his parents in massive murderous debt
from his medical bills and special expenses. Some say
lil jimmy was a selfish fellow with a "ME" complex.
"buy 'ME' a wheelchair.
"'I' need more medicine."
"'I'M' in a lot of pain."
Always thinking of himself lil jimmy was.
(actually it was his grandfather that insisted we
cremate his remains so no one else could catch
the incurable shit that little jimmy had.)
but enough about the good times, lets talk about the facts.
(And we could probably capitalize the "j" in his
name throughout this poem, but, come on, does it
really matter? I mean let's call a spade a spade.
It's not like lil jimmy is going to complain. Right?) Facts.
ANYWAY
Lil jimmy loved Dicks. He begged to meet Dicks, he
wanted to play with Dicks. He wanted to sleep with
Dicks. Lil jimmy just loved Dicks. Now I could go on
and on, but I think we gave jimmy enough time from
our lives already. He's dead. And his love of Dicks
didn't save him. The Dicks couldn't save him.

No Dick can.
So let's focus on the moral of this story.

'If you're sick, you might die.'

Lil jimmy did. His shit fucking killed him. Oh yeah,
the hospital burned down his fucking room too.

<u>Good Head</u>

There are many things that have names that shouldn't,
or may be questionable. I'm no food constable, but
for instance, lets start with what's on the table.
Why do they call it a head of lettuce? Is
it able to speak?Sometimes it's shredded,
then what? Is it then a treat?
I could line my underwear with it and it could become
a cold ass-tasty fetish that smells like balls and
dickmeat. Just saying, don't blame me for playing the
game they make up in some office dictating what I'm
to say about the vegetation on the dinner table!
I mean, I could use it as a ball and chain or give it a
mouth some eyes and a brain. I can toss it around
and call it Wilson or plant it in my yard and watch
it grow. Maybe I'll carve out two eye holes and fuck
those sockets slow. Who the fuck knows. You named
it, not me, it was just a green thing until you gave
it it's fame to be something it didn't have to be.

Maybe I should crack it open slow and eat it like a prison
inmate eats ass and vagina on his last day before they
fry him like donuts in the frytub. Then the coroner is
fucked, and has to open him up like a casserole, pulling
out shreds of heads of lettuce out of his dead asshole, what
a hassle. Maybe I'm just an asshole thinking too hard
about my gastrointestinal ass flow, maybe I should just
shut the fuck up, ignore what's in my head, buy the dam
thing with no regrets and eat it with a light vinaigrette.
There, enough said. It's a head.

Breathless & Homeless

I never wanted to be this way, a nuisance, living in fear.
I'm pretty sure very few, if any, aspire to be here. It
wasn't a plan or a goal to have no where to go. I thought
I did everything I was supposed to; school, chores, smile
politely, join the military and move on, but somehow here
I am, alone and dragged down by a few different things,
mainly my own hand, I get that and I can absolutely accept
that. However that doesn't change the fact of where I am.
I don't feel like repeating myself.
I'm just out of breath. I fucked up and this is where I am,
holding my head in my hands, regurgitating old plans.
This chair where I sit and stare into the wonder of my
failures and man are there so many, isn't even mine.
I don't own a thing except the clothes on my back,
in fact, I think the jacket is borrowed
and I have to give it back.
My friends are few and far between. I've survived on
the bottom for so long I wouldn't even know what a
real life looked like if it rose up and showed itself.
The money I make is abysmal. My name is a surprise
to those who remember my existence, their response
isn't even worth mentioning. I had talents and they've
gone to waste, I tried and fell apart at that critical
stage and now I'm left to watch, a lifetime pass before
me uneventfully. No one's proud of me. I don't have
any family. I've done nothing historically. I'm going
nowhere. I'm hungry, lonely, numb and not dying fast
enough to get past the suffering, what's left for me?
It's been a tragedy to watch myself fall apart in front of me.
I feel like crying, but I remember, it was never a remedy...

...How can any man feel alone in a world full of billions of people. How anyone can turn their back on another brother is beyond me, yet men, women and children are suffering. Yes, our sibling souls. Homelessness exists, it's all around us, reach out and make a difference, don't just stand there and watch, they're regular people, our brothers and sisters, who've hit rockbottom after getting the wind knocked out of them. I know, cuz I've been there personally and I've had hands reach down and pull me up off my knees. Thankfully, I was lucky.

Losing Faith

I was losing faith faster than I could save me.
Losing faith in myself, even spiritually.
I know we all go through this at some point, but at no
point does that fact rescue us from the darkness.

I've always been a simple man;
food, home, maybe a couple bucks, see my kids,
occasionally a stroke of good luck, and something
for my heart. After all that's been torn apart, I just
wanted a little something for the best parts of me.
A woman, a bond, moments of clarity with a deserving
entity. A good soul to fill the emptiness inside me with a
genuine love that could grow if we took care of it just so.

I became jaded, cynical, unforgiving, and unstable.
Emotional, angry, hostile, feeling terrible,
and then I met her.
It was a long wait and a lot of pain consumed
my days but I found myself smiling again.
So this passage is not to God or my new love,
this is for myself in case I ever forget.

I don't ever want to see that broken man in the mirror
again. Love this woman with every fiber of your being,
I had no idea this is what it feels like to be living.

You Ain't Shit **

It's shocking that you're still doubting me, like I'm some
kind of moron spitting idiocy. Honestly, you need a
lobotomy. Shit's pent up inside of me, just waiting to get
outta me, and it's flowing like Shakespeare's diary, but for
some reason it's not good enough for your high society,
high and mighty intellect. But if I recollect, and don't
neglect to correct if I misdirect as I reflect, but the bed you
made has never left us amazed. You're words are tired,
you're a boring haze, fading fast, a pathetic blast from
the past. You're arthritic, you're passe at best and while
we're on the subject, you look like shit. That's not a cheap
shot, it's truth to the crock pot of crap that don't stop.
Please, lock up your mouth,
you're not, stocked in clout,
you're rock-bottoming out,
you're being, phased the fuck out,
you act like you're, from down south;
three biscuits and a bucket of chicken,
you couldn't suck a dick with someone elses mouth.

So next time please, don't talk shit in an others
direction, that's just a limp wristed, feeble attempt
with a limp dick erection to get attention.

The Tale of the Miserable Fuck *

This is the tale of the miserable fuck. Just a short story
about a real prick. A piece of work in every way. He would
talk shit about everyone under his breath, every fucking
day. This fake ass piece of miserable shit betrayed and
played as if he was doing the right thing by ratting every
chance he got, about anything that seemed off to him, no
matter what. He overstepped his position and made an
opposition of every man around him because everything
had to be his way.

One day a patient man, a saint as he was known,
recognized the traits of the old miserable, cock sucking
bag of bones and tried a new angle. He approached
him with kindness and gestures and invitations to
family dinners- suspecting the miserable fuck had no
one left to love, no one to share life with or even speak
of. Of course the saint's suspicions were true. That old
miserable fuck had lost everything he ever knew. He
became injured and depressed, not a woman nor a child
or even a friend would ever come through. So the saint
continued his mission of kindness with belief that one
day through the years, the old man would be brought
to tears and see the error in his ways. Well, after many
years of hellos and good mornings, gifts and genuine
greetings, the saint had reached a point to speak about
his humanitarian connection and called a meeting.

"Gather 'round good gentlemen, I have something to
say, as God is my witness on this very day, I've done my
very best to find a better way to communicate and after
years of hard work that I did so dedicate, it's my job as a
saint to tell you all what I've learned before its too late.
He's not a miserable fuck. Please don't call him that,
He's a gargantuan, miserable fucking cunt. I've tried
everything except shooting him in the face. There's
no hope for that bigoted piece of dog shit disgrace.

42

He's an absolute backstabbing backwards twit. A know it all, sac of monkey shit. A moron without brain "one" in his fucking head and there's zero chance to connect with him cuz he's most likely inbred. Let's all pray that miserable fuck falls down a flight of stairs, breaks every bone in his body and dies today. God bless everyone, except that miserable fuck and have a great day.

The Adventures of Dickstain
& Captain Fuckstick **

We find our heroes wandering through a foreign
land, searching for sustenance so grand, it
was said to be out of fucking hand.
"Don't touch anything Dickstain." said the older brother.
"Don't worry I won't Fuckstick! I'm just looking for
something. Something I know is here or was in tale. It
was said to be red and green with mighty purple hairs."
He said as they tip-toed with extreme care, for they were
in the lair of the pig nosed, cow-bellied momma bear.
"Wow. Red and green. I bet that's quite a mean...
Shhh! I hear someone coming. Quick Dickmeat, hide."
"Don't call me that, I'm not a queer."
"Whatever Dickstain. I have no doubt
you take it in the rear."
"Oh, good one Captain Fuckstick, did you stay up all
night thinking that one up? Now shut the fuck up and
look for a shiny tin. It holds the treasure we seek. The
treasure of pleasure that reeks beyond measure. An aroma
so alluring it's captives fall under it's spell. I'm talking
about the fabled deer frozen in headlights look. A tight
as fuck alien abduction of epic proportion. The reason
Pink Floyd is on the moon and Led is in the Zepplin."
"Hark! I found the tin. It's under Momma bear's
fatass chin, along with some percocets."
"Be sure not to wake the bitch, she'll rip off our nuts
and throw us in a ditch. Quick, take what we need and
leave the rest under her saggy-ass, dilapidated breasts.
I can't stand the shriek of shock of us in her nest. Last
time she caught me, she made me her cleaning bitch,
fuck that shit. Hey... Fuckstick, do we even have fire?"

44

"Don't worry about me Dickstain, I brought a pipe
and a light. I wish you'd give me some fuckin'
credit. Tonight we go out in a blaze of glory.
We'll be higher than fuck 'til morning.
Now let's get out of here before we get caught.
End of fucking story."

Space Ace & Monkey **

Come in Space Ace, come in. This is ground control, the
only post that has your last communication. We also
know you're a dumb ass fool for taking this mission
instead of vacation. So listen. This station, hasn't heard
from you. It's day thirty-two. These men still have jobs
to do. Contact us soon or we're assuming you're losing
speed and you're off course; gone forever, wait, it gets
worse. You're lost together, left the ship and severed
your tether and whether you've followed your notes to
the letter all for the better, you're taking measures to
adjust. There's emergency levers if you must, so get it
together and remember, it's Jupiter's moons or bust.

Now, this office is a hot box full of soft cocks wearing
black socks, eatin' tuna outta zip-locks, with bad
breath readin' desktops, sweatin like chicks wearing
crop tops in the back drop. But they're not. This is
serious and I mean this, you're approaching Venus
with only one engine working and it's freezin',
so believe me- you need us.

"This is Space Ace. I hear you loud and clear. You won't
believe what happened here. My circuits got fried when
Monkey pulled out his jungle dick and pissed inside
the capsule, ruining the module. He's a real asshole.
He ate all the food, took a shit and flung his poo into
my eye. I cried tears of shit and now I'm flying blind.
Who's idea was it to put a monkey in the sky by my
side. I can hear him jacking off and smiling as I vomit
in my helmet from the stench of hot monkey shit. I'll
be home real soon but first I'm dropping off that hairy
prick and his lumps of floating poo, on the moon."

Blossom **

Dick biscuit, fuck-stick and cunt-lick cannot be used to
describe your grandmother. Limp-dick, skin-flap and sac-
dragger are not to be used to address your grandfather. But
we all know about your whore of a mother, who brought
joy to so many others from shore to shore, making sure
she sucked every dick so pure as if they all had the cure.
She wanted nothing more than to be good in bed, and
with a nickname like Red, how could she not be. She was
always cock-heavy, a half lesbian lefty, a seasoned veteran,
who let them all in. With a club foot and a pending
hysterectomy, she used to beg me with that banged up
pussy, that hung three inches below where it should be,
to come over and stuff her like a thanksgiving turkey.
I declined all except one time...
and that's why you call me Daddy.

The Stork and the Ho *

Lisa was quite the Ho, well, with a name like Lisa, that's
already known. Lisa didn't care about consequences.
She would sleep with any man that crossed her path
that made promises. Throw a drink in with that and
a guy could play all day. At the ripe age of twenty
three Lisa cried in pain and begged for mercy. No,
not from S.T.D's, although she has been extremely
lucky; she had never given thought to pregnancy, until
now. News traveled fast as the stork caught wind of
her baby bump. He ran to the head stork up front.
"There's no way I'm giving that whore a kid,
she doesn't even have a home, and sucked
fourteen dicks this Tuesday alone!"
The head stork stood and said,
"Well you better get this resolved, 'cuz in no
time she'll be next on your delivery list- unless
you can prove she's outright wrong for the task,
in which case we'll give the father the kid."
On a mission, the stork called in a favor; his
friend the beaver and a donkey, his neighbor.
"Guys, I need you to let me know if that Ho
can handle this gift. If she does one more sexual thing
while this pregnancy is in, the whore ain't gettin' a kid,
the father is."
Some time had passed and the Stork went to check on
his buddies and see how they were doing. He wanted
to film her wrongful pleasures and found quite the
goings on. Lisa had become friends with the two, but the
donkey blocked the view. All he heard were the words,
"I love petting my hairy beaver and rubbing my fat ass too."
But that wasn't enough to convict. He had to
catch her in the act, catch her sucking on a
dick. So the stork flew in for a closer look.

48

That's when he tripped over the donkeys cock,
stepped on the hairy beaver and landed in her
nook. The donkey kicked and shook his fat ass,
while the beaver danced in the gook. Seems the
stork landed dick first, fell into her pussy fat and
accidentally fucked her in the kid crack.
The beaver was so shocked he yelled,
"Get a lawyer, 'cuz in about two minutes you'll
be a dirty ass, whore fucking, father!"

The Worth of a Modern Man

Days run into years where he never takes a stand. He
carries the frustration of failure like heavy baggage on
a plane that never lands. Doomed if he lets it linger,
doomed if he speaks of the monster. No one would listen
or want to hear the cross cries of an angry father.
He's a crazy man, they say. Insane, unreliable again.
His warnings are mocked and the failures
that befall his flock are all his fault. He's the
only one to blame. if only that were true.
Because he'll wear those ribbons of shame and endure the
pain that he knows only he can handle as he's cast out and
branded. It comes with the territory of caring for a family.
He won't tell you, he knows it's his
job to protect and shield you.
Every person has their point of view.
Nevertheless that truth is ignored and ripped up
like dead infected roots that need to be removed,
as not to poison the others around him.
To be treated like this astounds him.
His views, his thoughts and existence are obscene,
pointless, nothing less and demeaned.
He's the pariah that never should've been.

Misunderstood, mistreated, misdiagnosed and
deceived by those he believed in.
Misplaced like a mere trinket from a trip,
long forgotten. In time he rots until he's worthless.
Taken for everything he's got, taken for granted.
Used til he's useless. Abused til he dies and is no longer
a burden. Don't worry, you've already hurt him.

Now drain the fuck out of him til he's down on his knees,
stand there and watch him bleed, then talk to him like
he didn't just carry you all through the dark, in his arms,
through all the scary parts, lighting the way with his heart.

This is obscene.

Seriously

Seriously bro?
you gotta be fucking kidding.
This is utterly embarrassing, it's disgusting,
you've crossed a line, and I'm protesting.
I shouldn't have to say this,
but someone has to...
you smell like a giant pile of cow shit and tobacco.
It's like you're smoking your own shit
then blowing it out your asshole.
It's like your mother breastfed you rancid
tit milk through rotting goat dick.
I've never smelled skin so putrid.
Honestly, I wanna punch your mother square in the
face for being so useless. Don't get too close to the
rest of us. I can't even breathe near you, my lungs
literally close up in fear when I hear you. It must
be a self defense mechanism. This isn't criticism.
You smell like you bathed in a hot piss baptism.
I can't even believe you got hired.
Go set your clothes on fire.... with you in them.
Your armpits smell like a monkey fucked a fish,
your breath is a death sentence, like you just ate a dog shit
sandwich then sucked an elephants dick. It's so fucking
bad I could be blind and still know your distance.
Either you're a lazy a piece of shit or you're flat
out retarded, but no one can be this clueless.
You're a walking diseased health hazzard.
Go home and scrub something, you filthy
bastard. Anything, with bleach. Shave every shit
covered rank hair, and wash your fucking puke
scented feet. And don't forget your balls.
I'm sure they're absolutely vomit inducing.
You need to be quarantined, that's all.
And then of course, shot in the fucking face. You're
a disgrace and an embarrassment to the race.

Silhouette

I don't want to just tell a story or magnify personal
traits for the sake of glory in how I'll be perceived
by pretentiously delivering a poetic piece.
Nor do I want to come across preachy like I'm teaching
you anything, as if I believe wholeheartedly, I'm
reinventing the wheel of advice, common sense and
self deliverance.
I just want what we all want when we wake up and look in
the mirror since we were young, wondering who we are,
who am I, what am I, what's my purpose, will I be of, and
am I of any importance to the existence of mankind in this
majestic, epic saga called 'life' in it's grand display. Can
I be more than a just another shadow cast in the day?

I watch complacency get the best of us and for some,
to overcome and become more than an empty human
hollow, that consumes and follows, is asking people
not to be lazy and settle, but to test your mettle and
strive for a higher level than the low bar they've
set for themselves. It's incredible, even terrible,
"If it's meant to be" is another awful excuse and a diluted
down delusion of truth to use as the reason they poison
their existence without resistance and fallback instead of
reaching for the challenges of being all you can be, making
your mark with something that will carry on in dreams
and memories. Some of us don't shine as bright as others,
but you still have to try to be more than just another
number on a front door. Stand up and stand out, be heard,
let your voice break the curse. Sing your song, write your
story, create glory and dream big, because there's more
to this than we think. Life deserves for us to be loud.
Be more than just a silhouette in the crowd.

Printed in the United States
By Bookmasters